Restaurant Marketing

Tips & strategies to win in the Food Business

Restaurant Marketing

Tips & strategies to win in the Food Business

By

Robert Mark Jakobsen

Publisher: BoD – Copenhagen, Denmark
Printing: BoD – Norderstedt, Germany

ISBN: 978-87-7170-430-3

Contents

Introduction

It isn't just the quality of your food, your location, or the friendliness of your staff which will help you succeed. The key to a growing restaurant business is marketing. It generates revenue, and there are lots of easy and low-cost marketing tactics that will help any restaurant grow into a valuable asset.

Most restaurants don't focus enough on marketing, so a little of the advice in this book will go a long way. Even picking a handful of ideas and trying them out is sure to get extra customers through the door and make a big difference to your profit levels.

We'll look at how you can increase sales inside the restaurant, online and on social media, and some of the important things to remember when you're starting up. Next we'll take a quick peek at your brand and image and how to improve it, and then onto the people and personalities you need to interact with to succeed.

Never forget that restaurants are primarily people businesses, not food businesses, and it's your charm, professionalism and positivity which will help you build relationships, not fancy cooking.

The next topic is restaurant growth, which is a short introduction to the numbers behind the business, and how you can fine tune the parts of your business to maximize profits. Finally, for those who are rushed off their feet and need some rapid inspiration, I've put together some top tip lists with

Inside The Restaurant

Rethink Your Menu

Your restaurant menu is the most important tool inside the restaurant. You should make sure your menu is neat, and easy to read with a simple font, clear descriptions and clear pricing. Restaurant customers generally remember the first and the last items listed in the menu, so put your best food in these premium slots. Another trick is to show off your three most profitable items in a box. As you learn more about profit margins, cut out the low profit items from the menu.

Foodie Photos

The very best way to visually promote your food is high quality, mouth wateringly setup photos. Taking great food photos can be more difficult than it seems. If you can find a good deal, you could hire a professional photographer to take some top-notch photos of both the food and the restaurant itself. You'll use these time and again in publicity, menus, websites and online, and a good picture is worth a thousand words. It can also be helpful for people who don't speak English to have something they can see when ordering.

Loyalty Programs

Join online restaurant sites, deal sites like and sign up for food apps and it consider as a part of restaurant marketing plan. Online apps always help your visitors by giving them access to discounts, deals and loyalty programs. It also helps visitors to offer a discount for visiting your restaurant a certain number of times. Many restaurants use a stamped card, it's simple, cheap and very effective in drawing people back in.

Regular Customers

Increase customer loyalty is one of the top marketing goals to improve your restaurant profit. Regular customers are the most profitable because they already demonstrated they like what you offer, and it doesn't cost money in marketing to bring them in. If you have 20-30 regular customers then your business will always profitable.

Host Events

Putting on an event like a tasting, a champagne evening, special Valentines menu, or Xmas and New Year extravaganza can attract new customers and give regulars a reason to come back. With a little thought you can come up with an overall concept, then do some basic marketing to advertise it. Maybe distribute a few fliers and send a free press release to the local media. If it's a really lavish event, or something unusual you could also try local television stations.

Deliveries

People are often too busy with no time to cook but they also might not want to go out to eat. Implementing a delivery system needs a little thought, some planning and transportation but it's another marketing channel and an additional revenue stream. Your packaging should remind customers about your business, keep the food warm and project a high quality image. Print takeout or delivery menus and distribute them around the town with promotions people or you can also distribute them door-by-door by post. Only include items in the delivery menu that are easily transportable.

Go Green

Nowadays around 70% of regular restaurant customers say that they look for eco-friendly restaurants. Green food and environmentally friendly policies can bring lots of customers to your business but you need to do it right. Look at recycling, what you do with food waste, and contact some local environmental groups for advice. You can also look for sustainably produced ingredients.

Online Marketing Tips for Restaurants

Now a day's most of people use the internet and a restaurant customers in particular use search engines and customers review site s to find restaurants. A customer usually wants to see the menu before visiting and may want to know about the wine list, the chef and the ambiance before he books a table.

Today's restaurants do more online marketing than traditional advertising. You can do a quick Google search to find the same type of restaurants as yours and compare both your websites and also how easy it was to find them. This is a great first step with online marketing – basic research that will tell you a lot about the local market.

<u>A Basic Website</u>

One of the best ways to market your restaurant is simply using your website. More than 80% Americans have internet access and it's growing day by day. More than 50% of adults use the internet to choose restaurants, so that's a huge online market without even considering social media.

Your website doesn't need to be a huge, complex affair, as long as it looks good, explains your food and beverage offerings, shows off your premises with a few photos and has a map, opening hours and contact information – it's a good start. If you don't have time to build a website you can always outsource it.

It should be very easy to access this basic information, but you can go further with online bookings, reviews, scanned newspaper articles on the restaurant and information about your background, staff and attitude to food and eating out.

<u>Search Engine Optimisation</u>

If your customers can't find you or your site, you're website isn't working hard enough. A well optimized website will feature in searches for your type of food and your local area. You can check this with a few simple Google, Bing and Yahoo searches. What page of the results do you show up on? Search engine optimization requires proper keywords and content on your site, and some knowledge of how companies like Google rank pages.

Focus on making sure your written content, pictures and video is all relevant to your niche, and that you have plenty of good quality information online.
Search engines love content, they love unique content with keyword rich tags and content.

10 Ways To Indirectly Get To The Top Of Search Engines

This is what internet marketers do to get Indirectly get to the top of Search engines I hope it be an inspiration for you.

There are millions of web sites trying to get listed in the top 20 spots of the major search engines. That amounts to a lot of competition! I say if you can't get listed at the top, indirectly get to the top.

How do you do this? Look up the top 20 web sites on the major search engines under the keywords and phrases people would find your web site. The key would be to then advertise on those web sites.
The most expensive way would be to buy ad space on those web sites. If you don't want to spend any money, you could use the ten strategies below. These strategies may not apply to every web site.

1. Participate on their discussion boards. You could post questions, answer other peoples questions, and join in on conversations. Just include your signature file and link at the end of your messages.

2. Ask the web site owner if they would like a free ebook to giveaway to their visitors. You could have them link to your web site or include your ad in the free ebook.

3. Submit content to their web site. You could write articles for their web site and include your resource box and link at the end of the article. If they publish it, you'll indirectly be at the top of the search engines.

4. Write an excellent article review of their web site, products or services. Then publish the review on your web site. E-mail the web site owner and tell him or her about it. They may link to your web site so their visitors read it.

5. Ask the owner of the web site if they would want to trade advertising. If you don't get as much traffic as they do, you could throw in some extra incentives.

6. Propose a cross promotion deal with the web site. You both could promote each others products or services together in one package deal. This means a mention and link back to your web site.

7. Give the web site a testimonial for their product or service. Include a little text link for your web site with the testimonial. You never know; it could end up on their ad copy.

8. Post your advertisement on their free classified ad section on their web site. You want to be sure you have an attractive headline so they will read your ad.

9. Post your text link on their free-for-all links page. You want to go back and post your link regularly so it stays towards the top.

10. Sign their guest books. You could leave a short compliment about their web site on their guest book. Just include your signature file and link at the end ofyour message.

Partner Sites

Food is huge online and from blogs, cooks and competitions to listings sites, entertainment guides and cuisine websites there are always people you can partner with online. Try offering a free meal to popular bloggers if they'll review your restaurant, and try emailing a selection of relevant sites to see if they'll exchange links or promote you in some way.

Grow Your Email Database

You can never have enough good quality emails in your database. Email direct marketing is free, and the bigger your database, the more people who will respond to your marketing. Like expanding your marketing territory, growing your email database makes the numbers game work in your favour. Collect emails through your website, on customer comment cards and through business card collecting and local research.

Freshen Up Your Menu

Your online menu should be as easy to read as your printed menu. Many restaurants think their online menu is an afterthought, but actually, especially for functions and group bookings, reading up about your restaurant's offering online is crucial. Make sure all the information and prices tally with your print menu, add your drinks list, and any special dishes of the day or offers. Consider getting a PDF menu made which people can email around.

Manage Your Online Reputation

Business reviews are now an essential part of any business because the internet makes it easy to post and view opinions. You should always keep your eye on customer reviews. 90% of internet users read online reviews which influence their buying decisions. One negative review can slow your business growth. Too many negative reviews can really negatively impact your business. So always try to keep your customers happy and be organized in responding to problems. Ask your customers to write reviews and make sure you, or your staff respond to negative reviews and make amends for bad customer experiences if they occur.

Email and SMS Marketing

With direct marketing you can promotions, deals and incentives right to customers through email, SMS, and even phone calls. Direct marketing only works if you keep customers' contact information in into your restaurant database. Even if you just use a guest book to take details you'll build up an invaluable resource over time. The more you can collect information on customers the more you can market your business so it fits their needs. For example, just knowing their date of birth gives you a shot at hosting their birthday party if you send a card at the right time.

Set Up Google Alerts

Google alerts inform you when your business name appears on other web sites. It makes it easy to know who is talking about your business and it lets you spot new opportunities automatically. It's a free service and takes only seconds to setup.

Blogging

You can start your own blog free of charge and it takes only a moment to get going. Blogging is great because it . You can share your success, struggles, funny moments, recipes and anything which people might find interesting.

Social Media Marketing for Restaurants

Restaurant owners always need to engage with their customers. Social media is a cheap way to engage and build relationships, try out new ideas and promotions and also get valuable feedback from customers and people who might visit.

<u>Facebook Marketing-</u>

Facebook gives outstanding opportunity to a business to get increase customers day by day by making regular postings, of both text and photos. You can include delicious food photos and pictures of customers, as well as special offers, deals and new menus. Facebook does demand a bit of time and effort, because posts and longer and the site has many more options than Twitter for example. It's a long term game plan you need to follow, gradually building up the number of Likes for your page, and interacting with people over time.

Facebook also offers paid advertising. This can be good if you're just starting out or need an immediate boost for an event.

<u>Twitter Marketing-</u>

Twitter is a very useful marketing tool for restaurants. It allows only 140 characters per post so your messages have to be quick and punchy. You can include links in your tweets and drive traffic to your website through the use of hashtags, following other Twitter users and making posts. Twitter is probably less time consuming than Facebook thanks to the limit format, but it needs special skill to keep things shorts and sweet.

You also offers targeted ads. If your restaurant is located in Seattle for example then you can fine tune your ad posts so it covers your particular part of that area.

Starting Up

If you have dreams of opening a restaurant then get thinking. Lack of planning is the biggest reason for failure for most businesses. Here are some top tips for starting up a successful restaurant business.

<u>Planning</u>

First and foremost, think about all the sacrifices you'll have to make. It's important to prepare mentally to open a restaurant. It's hard work, the hours are long and antisocial and there is a lot of pressure because your reputation is on the line every day. It's also hard to earn money, and it's more of a passion than a business for most successful owners.

Second, do your research and make a proper business plan. Look at your competitors, your target audience, how you'll do marketing and most importantly how you will balance your budget.

Location matters in the restaurant business. You need to select a location where crowds gather, and people pass by. At the same time you need to select location which can fits within your budget. Its hard to find a perfect spot for a new business, because the more passing trade there is, the more the rent will be. It's a question of committing to the search and taking your time to make a decision.

You may have lots of dishes you love for your new restaurant but you need to test them before you serve them to your customers. Try them out on friends and family, and even staff. Get as many opinions as possible and ask yourself questions. Can the chef cook each dish in a reasonable time? How much does each dish cost, and what is the profit margin on each?

A restaurant relies on great staff to run well. To have staff, you must have a manager if you don't have time to look after the little details. For many owners it can be overwhelming trying to go it alone. A good manager can help and train staff, liaise between waiters and the kitchen, welcome customers and deal with accounts and suppliers, leaving you free to work on the wider picture and overall strategy.

<u>Funding</u>

Before you start your business you make sure that how much money you can spend on your business, how much money you need to live, and how long you can survive before profits come in. Your restaurant will take time to earn a profit. It will not be profitable from day one and many owners have to finance their restaurant through a bank loan or savings. You must sacrifice lots of your time and energy, so plan accordingly and make sure that your ideas will not go over budget.

<u>Managing</u>

Managing means so many things, it's impossible to cover everything in this introduction. From a marketing perspective, as the owner, you're where the buck stops. If you don't see improvements to your finances after you've advertised or done publicity work, you've done something wrong, and it's important to see where you went wrong so next time you get a proper return on investment. It's also important to look at long term marketing goals. A little and often should be your mantra.

<u>Stay Up To Date</u>

A restaurant owner must always be up to date on market trends, facts, statistics etc. It can help you to analyze the market and create a forward thinking marketing plan. Market trends can help you to spot opportunities in growing sectors and avoid niches which are in decline. It's all about staying ahead of the curve and not getting caught out.

Branding & Image

Many business owners believe that word of mouth is the best promotion tool for any restaurant, and they're right. Word of mouth today means more than verbal recommendations. It can come through social media in an instant, and it can work gradually when you build an online buzz. It's all about atmosphere, image and branding, and the harder you work at these, the more word of mouth you'll get. You must have great food, great atmosphere, clean toilets, good music and great staff, but you need more than that. You need a brand experience.

From the style of your furniture to your logo, people make judgements about your restaurant as soon as they see or hear things.

<u>Choose A Great Name</u>

You need to choose a name which is easy to remember, easy to spell and if possible try to choose the name which has a compelling background story. If you want to open a seafood restaurant for example, there are plenty of myths, legends, films and classic cultural words you can draw on for inspiration. It's not easy to choose a name which can attract your customers and which you also like personally, it's rather like naming a baby, but in the end your name will become a vital part of your identity.

What's Your Story?

Everyone loves a good story, and your story in the restaurant trade is another key part of your brand. If you grew up learning recipes from your parents, or if you travelled the world working as a chef and now decided to open your own place, your journey is important. People aren't just coming to eat with you, they're coming for something different – a kind of entertainment, and explaining why you do what you do is all theatre.

Develop Brand Identity

Your restaurant brand identity is built around your restaurant, your food, your prices and service and the picture people form of you from your marketing. Do you have a clear, minimalist interior and a simple, modern menu, or are you traditional, with heavy furniture, hearty food and a long, descriptive menu? Consider just your logo. Is it funky and fun, or cool and sophisticated? Try to see your brand identity through the eyes of a customer.

One of the first things you can do to develop your brand identity is get a graphic designer to come up with some different looks for your menu, logo and signage. Try them out on family and friends and get some feedback on which works best. You can also do this with your interior with 3D design programs which let you model new styles in the virtual world. This can help you fine tune your space before you have to spend a cent on decorating.

Hotels and Tourist Agencies

If your restaurant is located near tourist agencies or hotels you can contact their managers and ask them to refer people to you. You'll need to offer them something in exchange, like free dinners or drinks, but this usually works very well for everyone involved.

Food Festivals

Food festivals are the perfect platform to promote your restaurant. You check for dates in your area and in most cases it's just a question of filling out an application and getting ready for the food festival. It's a chance to mingle with other restaurateurs, and see what other cuisines are popular in the area.

You can give away samples, run a special tasting menu, or even show people how you make your dishes in an interactive cookery class. There will usually also be giveaways and prizes so you can put up some gift vouchers to take part.

Local Ingredients

Customers love to eat local foods because it's the freshest way from farm to plate, and there are huge environmental benefits too as well as economic benefits for the local community. It's all part of the 21st century restaurant experience and creating positive buzz. Search for suppliers at farmers markets and online and look for specialist shops who might have local contacts.

Signature Dishes

In large cities there are lots of places to eat. So if you want to attract customers to your restaurant then you need to cook up some signature items and unique treats no-one else has. No need to cook everything as like signature item but to be become a famous restaurant you need to cook two or three items and mark it as premium quality food. You can showcase these items to the local media, social networks and food websites. It's a way of showing what you can do, grabbing attention and creating a premium brand.

Get good Google reviews

This input from www.restaurant-website-reviews.toptenreviews.com

Offer Some Background – Be sure to offer as much information about the restaurant you are reviewing as possible, including location, phone number, type of cuisine, hours, etc. On many restaurant review websites you must add the restaurant to the site database (if it is not already there) and fill in any information the site asks for (like whether or not the restaurant serves alcoholic beverages or takes reservations). If another user posted inaccurate information – such as the wrong hours – change the information yourself or inform the website directly.

Give Both Pros and Cons – Maybe the food was less than stellar but was the service unparalleled? If your restaurant experience was riddled with both pros and cons, make sure you list both to provide readers with an accurate, well-rounded review.

Name Specific Entrees – Most restaurant-goers will appreciate specific recommendations and whether or not you loved or hated the food. Listing specifically what you ordered will help validate your opinions. Some review websites even have a spot where you can list exactly what dishes you ordered.

Evaluate the Entire Experience - While the food is obviously the main attraction of any restaurant, there are other factors that can greatly influence the overall dining experience including ambiance, décor and service are important to note. For example, how quickly did you receive your food and was the server attentive to your needs? Did the décor enhance or distract from the overall ambiance of the restaurant? Be specific as possible about the details of the restaurant.

Use Descriptive Adjectives – To really spice up your review (no pun intended), use descriptive adjectives. For example, instead of simply saying that the grilled chicken you ordered was "bad," tell why it was bad; was it dry, bland, too salty, etc? Rest assured, you can never provide too much detail in a restaurant review.

Let Your Personality Shine Through – No one wants to read a boring, dull review of anything, let alone a restaurant. Furthermore, there is no added value or insight to your review if you simply copy what someone else has already written. Make your review highly personal and unique to you, using your own "voice;" readers will be much more interested and find your review helpful if it is genuine

Personality & People

The people and personalities who visit, work and deal with the restaurant are really at the very core of what it means to be a restaurateur. Keeping everyone happy while maintaining boundaries and professionalism is a tricky balancing act. It pays not to be overfriendly, but then you don't want to come off as too distant.

Dealing with people the right way comes with practice. If you're shy or have trouble with strangers, the only way to deal with this is to force yourself to interact. Over time, your confidence will develop and you'll be able to handle even raucous parties and large unruly groups with ease.

Perhaps the best advice is to be yourself. Customers quickly see through false fronts so be natural and encourage your staff to be natural too. There's nothing wrong with a few nerves provided you're honest and open.

<u>Know Thy Customer</u>

Get to know your customers, both as individuals and as social groups. Who are the business people? Who are the families? Who orders what? How much does each group spend. You should also get to know people personally, find out their tastes and interests. Customers need to feel like you and your staff are making an effort with them socially. Make sure employees know to remain polite even if customers get difficult or a situation becomes tense. A cool, friendly approach always calms customers down and lets problems get solved faster.

Treat Customers Like Family

From the minute customers approach your restaurant, treat them like honoured guests. That means opening the door to welcome them, leading them over to a table promptly, taking their order gracefully and dealing with issues quickly. Little gestures can make a big difference. For example, if a customer has spent a lot on his meal, why not offer him a free coffee or liquor as a thank you. Or if a group of friends is celebrating a birthday, help them by offering to bake a cake. Even something as minor as holding a customer's car door open and helping them out can make them feel like a rock star.

Train People Continually

You can train your employees continuously, give them help while they're working, sit them down after hours and brief them and keep adding to their skills and building their confidence. Don't let employees stagnate, you can always rotate them so that waiting staff work in the kitchen and vice versa from time to time. This keeps them aware of the business as a whole machine and helps them understand their part. You can also train staff to upsell and work for tips more effectively, driving up revenue.

Listen Carefully

Always listen to your customers. It's easy for some restaurant owners and managers to ignore customers on the grounds they know more, but this is a mistake. Your customers can tell you how to become more profitable, more popular and more successful better than anyone, so always look for feedback and act on it. Try customer comment cards, a personal goodbye from the manager, and emailed feedback forms to see which works best for you.

Promote Your Employees

If your managers or any stuff members come up with excellent ideas, reward them and see if you can put their idea into action. If you do this then staff will work harder and try to achieve the buzz of getting praise and seeing their thoughts change the restaurant for the better. The more you give, the more you can expect to receive. As well as promotions you can also award bonuses.

Keep An Eye On Everyone and Everything

Don't sit back and never think you're running a good business and it's time to start saving for a boat. It only takes a few minutes to kill the reputation that took years to earn. Keep your eye on things at all times, from the cash float and card receipts to drink levels, portion sizes and customer wait times for tables.

This also goes for any managers you have. The more trust and responsibility you give people, the more you have to check you're getting the results you deserve. That doesn't mean micro managing and constantly interfering, but it does mean making managers accountable. Often a regular meeting when you can discuss things privately is enough to keep most staff on their toes.

The Science of Restaurant Growth

Increase The Pool Of Possible Customers

You need more people to come and eat, and to do this you need to create the biggest possible pool of potential customers. For example, if you're currently advertising in one geographic area, and you add two new areas to your marketing activities – your marketplace has got bigger, and you have more chance of finding customers. Marketing is a numbers game, and widening your search and reaching out to more people multiplies all your other efforts and leads to more sales. It's as simple as that. So always look for new places to find customers.

Increase Your Profit Per Customer

Profits can be improved by either reducing your costs or increasing your margins. Cost reduction is beyond the scope of this book, but just think that replacing a paid newspaper ad with a press release which leads to a story will save you money on advertising which will become a bigger profit at the end of the day. There are lots of little ways to save, from changing suppliers to negotiating better deals and trimming unnecessary staff.

On the margin side, you'll need to think about pricing, test prices out at different levels and see whether you can encourage customers to order more when they visit. This is upselling, and it's all about adding value, giving people little extra treats they can't resist, and making visiting the restaurant more of an event. The perfect price for any item on the menu is one that is the maximum that's feasible while sales levels stay the same. This needs trial and error and a lot of experimentation.

Increase The Frequency Of Customer Visits

You must try to bring your customers back over and over again. Research has shown that keeping a hard core of regular clients, your restaurant will remain stable even in difficult market conditions. The key is innovation and staying in touch with customers. New menu items, new drinks, new deals and new events keep your restaurant fresh, and that's what draws people back. Of course, it's also a certain familiarity, so keep your most popular items on the menu at all times and try to find out from repeat customers what they love.

4 Core Ways to Increase Restaurant Sales

Get More People To Visit

Every business owner needs more customers to succeed, this isn't a secret and it seems obvious but many restaurant owners think they can sit back and wait for people to turn up. Restaurants are hyper competitive, so if you don't actively market yourself, other people will get the lion's share of the trade in your area. Put the time and effort needed into publicity.

Keep 'Em Coming Back

Once you get new customers to your business you must keep them coming back regularly. To do this you need to engage with them both inside the restaurant and outside the restaurant. As the business owner you must talk with the customers individually inside, and follow up with contact outside. Providing incentives and rewards for coming back regularly will help them feel valued.

Get Them Spending

Upselling means trying to increase each customer's overall spend. By offering drinks, extras, desert, coffee and liquors you are putting more options on the table, and encouraging customers to indulge. It's about suggesting, not selling, and it's crucial to train staff to be respectful and not pushy when they deal with customers.

Turn The Tables Quick

You need to reset the tables rapidly and prepare for the next guests as soon as customers leave their table. Your employees should never rush customers, but once they're gone, the sooner the table is filled, the better. With a bar area you can hold people waiting for a table, and with portable POS machines you can deal with payments anywhere you need to. The object is keeping customers flowing in and out smoothly.

8 Business Tips For Success

1. Learn how to cook, how to serve customers, and how to work at the bar or in the wine cellar. It's the only way to know every part of your business.

2. By eating in other restaurants of all types from budget to fine dining, you'll get ideas for you own, and you'll also learn about differences in customer service.

3. Always try to learn about your industry, read the trade magazines, follow trade and supplier blogs and keep up to date on social media about trends.

4. You can take business and accounting courses to create a business plan and keep track of your budget and finances more professionally.

5. Choose a great location which has great passing trade, and even consider moving if you're not in a good place. Location, location, location.

6. Make sure you have plenty of time to hire employees before launching your business. A six

month training period will help you to find quality employees.

7. You can start marketing your restaurant before open to the public, so plan ahead, because you can do early 'teaser' marketing and a campaign build up.

8. Never start restaurant business without a great chef, a great location and a great concept, these are the three most important assets to have.

Top 15 Quick Restaurant Marketing Ideas

If you're busy dealing with customers and suppliers, it can be easy to feel you don't have time to do marketing. In fact, there are many rapid fire fixes that can give you a little boost without needing a lot of commitment. Here's the top twenty, little ideas that go a long way and can be done in less than a day.

1. Check your social media and keep topping it up. Always retweet and reply to anyone who mentions your business. A few regular Tweets or Facebook posts can build you a useful social network over time.

   .

2. Respond to feedback left by your customers. If you get negative feedback be polite, always offer a refund or a voucher, and promise them to improve in future. Showing you care and you can take criticism generates goodwill.

3. Add photos of your new menu items, drinks and promotions to social media sharing sites like Instagram. You can also share pictures of special events, birthday parties and staff at work. You never know who might be looking.

4. Drop your business card at your local social hotspots. Take cards with you wherever you go, and be sure to exchange cards at parties and any kind of gathering. Put a box in the restaurant for business cards and draw one out each month for a prize.

5. Reward the first 20-30 people those who like your Facebook page. Give them 50% off, or a free bottle of wine, you'll more than make it up in increased turnover. The more you give, the more you're likely to get in the restaurant trade.

6. Promote your employees for helping you to do marketing. Encourage them to spread the word amongst family and friends and talk to new people they meet. Your staff are your publicity team and can make a big difference.

7. Invite people to a launch or re-launch party. People love and excuse to get out on the town, so give them one. You could also host a wine tasting or hook up with some musicians for a live music event.

8. Pay attention to your existing customers. Take a moment every day to walk round, talk and get to know their opinions and ideas about the restaurant. Encourage people to give you feedback and always act on their suggestions.

9. Keep your website updated. Many people let their website go stale, but this is usually the most important source of new customers. Is your menu and wine list up to date? Could you improve the information or the way it's presented?

10. Advertising your opening times. Make sure they are clearly displayed on your frontage, and also check directories and listings have the correct times. People get upset if you're closed when they think you're open, and vice versa.

11. Set up a page where customers can book online. Don't rely on customers to email or call, most are used to online booking systems for everything in their lives, so be sure your page is easy to use and confirms the booking properly.

12. Give video marketing a go. With a simple webcam and a little planning you could produce a short

video about your restaurant for You Tube. Videos are great because some customers don't read text websites, they only look for video.

13. Get out on the road to promote your restaurant. Visit the other restaurants, bars and hotels and see if you can find a way to partner with people in your area. Local networking is vital and you'll be surprised how many opportunities come your way as a result.

14. Try advertising in a local newspaper, perhaps using a coupon or special offer to draw people in. Just a simple ad can give you a lot of very targeted local publicity. Keep costs low, don't take out a full page, and measure the results you get.

15. Put your most profitable items at the top of the menu. This is the part most peoples' eyes are drawn to for the longest time, so keep your top sellers at the top. Another useful menu tip is making sure you have a range of food for all budgets.

Traditional Offline Marketing

Don't think of these methods as too simple or mundane. They are very effective when done right and combined with other techniques in this book.

Direct Mail – Nothing beats direct response when it comes to results-driven proven advertising. And messages sent directly to your highly targeted market via direct mail can deliver a terrific return on investment (ROI) when tested properly. There's a wealth of information on direct marketing by, Gary Halbert, Dan Kennedy, are some of many more experts.

Getting a deal with a big company customer can change the restaurants customer base radicle.

Postcards – Yes, postcards are a form of direct mail, but it warrants its own category. Postcards are cheaper to produce and mail than full-blown direct mail packages or sales letters, and they are great for generating leads and guest for you restaurant.
Postcards are also a great way to stay in touch with your customers and they also work well as part of a sequence of

mailings **Hint:** be sure to include yourself on the mailing list so you can get your own mailing as well.

Yellow Pages – Another great resource that is often underutilized or used ineffectively. Yellow page ads are great because when someone sees your ad, they are already in the market for your product or service. Yellow page ads need to be benefits-driven, with your Unique Selling Proposition (USP) stated clearly and boldly (remember, this is the one place where your prospects will see your ad alongside all of your competitors). You want your ad to stand out from the clutter. Use a direct response type of ad.

Flyers – Who says you can't hire a high school student to stuff mailboxes or stick 'em under windshields?

Networking – Your local Chamber of Commerce, BNI networking club, Sports club sponsor network and anywhere you have the opportunity to present your restaurant. In many cases, It's usually more effective to get you passion and ideas out to people verbally, so get your elevator speech ready and have plenty of business cards and special offers on hand.

Card Decks – These stacks of index cards are mailed to targeted audiences. Each deck can contain anywhere from 50 to 200 cards or so, each with an advertisement or coupon. They may also double as a business reply card on back. Since your ad is mixed in with tons of others, it's especially important to have a great headline and layout that will stand out from the clutter.

Card decks are inexpensive because all of the advertisers are sharing the cost of the mailing. They can cost as little as three cents a prospect for large mailings. Even for smaller mailings, they are generally cheap, which is good for testing your massage.

Value-Paks – Similar to card decks, "value-paks" are little booklets with multiple ads. They are mostly used with coupons, rather than business reply cards.

Gift Certificates – It's generally known that people will usually spend more than the gift certificate amount. So if you mail your customers a free no-obligation $15 gift certificate, it's usually a very sound investment. Most restaurant owners already know that people generally don't dine alone, so by giving your customers a free gift certificate, they're bound to bring in others who will spend more money on food and drinks. A good variation on this formula is the free birthday dinner. Generally, nobody is going to come in on their birthday and eat their free dinner by themselves. They're going to bring friends, relatives, you get the idea.

Here's a great way to use gift certificates to get referrals:
Send a letter to your customers with three gift certificates.
One they can use for themselves, and the other two they
can give away to friends or relatives. They keep your
customers happy (and happy customers are more likely to
speak highly of you to others) and they compound that fact
by letting your customers give the certificates to others, to
whom they will sing your praises.

Coupons – Like gift certificates, coupons are also a great
way to "touch" your customers and bring them back into
your store (or website or whatever).

Contests – The sandwich chain Subway recently had a
scratch-off contest, but you had to go online to see if you
were a winner. Contests are a great way to get leads and
generate sales. **Here's a tip:** always include an
unadvertised "second place" that everyone who didn't win
will get

Thank You Letters – Whether you send gift certificates,
coupons, a 2 for 1 special, a free gift, or just a friendly
thank you letter to stay on your customer's radar screen,
these types of letters are memorable and encourage your
customers to send you referrals. As always, these types of
letters should be personalized, and *never* use a mailing
address letter on the envelope.

Creative Business Cards – Besides using both sides of your
business cards and putting a compelling benefits-oriented

message on it, there are many other creative ways to put your business card to work for you. Of course, odd-shaped and "rolodex-styled" cards stick out from the crowd as well. One real estate agent in California hands an extra three bucks and a business card to the toll collector as he crosses the bridge into San Francisco. He tells the toll collector that he wants to pay for the driver behind him, and asks him to give the driver his business card. Nine out of ten times, the driver calls, at least to say thank you. He's sold several expensive homes that way as a result.

Ask Your Customers – It may sound super simple, but if you just ask your customers what they want and then give it to them, you'll be ahead of your competitors.

Do Research to Find Out What They Want – Again, this seems like a simplistic idea, but you'd be surprised how often it's overlooked.

Data-Based Marketing – Data-based marketing can be as simple as sending a greeting card or other "touch" communications with your customers and prospects.

You can build or use your booking system to build your database

Restaurants can do this all the time with the birthday gift certificates. Other companies take it a step further and know when their customers will need a reorder of their

product. They'll send a coupon or other discount to make another sale (for example, an oil change).
Nowadays with all of the "rewards" and "shopper's club cards," supermarkets and chain stores not only capture everything you purchase and when, they can send you coupons and discounts for those products you regularly purchase. Amazon sends you emails about books similar to ones you have purchased when they re released and during other promotions.

You may want to consider starting your own "rewards" type program or something similar.

Secret Sales – You can send your customers a postcard that has a secret discount from 10% to whatever on everything they buy in one visit. The catch is they have to come into your store to find out the amount of the discount. The chance that they may have a 75% off coupon, for example, is often irresistible to the customer.

Add Extra Amenities - For physical locations, such as a car dealership, consider testing an in-house diner, barber, coffee shop, putting green, wireless internet, video arcade, playrooms for children, book stores, manicurists, climbing walls, mini-museum, ice-cream shop, etc. These can work well especially for those businesses where their customers have to wait. It may sound extravagant, but many businesses, especially those that cater to the affluent, have done this with resounding success. Why do you think McDonalds added playgrounds to most of their restaurants? Why do upscale bookstores have coffee cafés? The list goes on.

Go to the "Edge" – Seth Godin talks about this in his book *Free Prize Inside*. Basically, the premise is that while your competitors sell to the "middle," you find ways to sell to the edge. It sets you apart from your competition, but it's not necessarily your USP. For example, the first release of that book came packaged in a cereal box with the prominent "Free Prize Inside" displayed.

Some more examples:

A massage salon moves their chairs outside in the summer.

A local pub built their own custom jukebox of twenty-six thousand songs in it by ripping their 1,798 CDs into a computer.

A restaurant in Manhattan makes the average Joe's wait, but gives the VIPs an unlisted number to get to the front of the line. Strangely enough, this pleases both groups (the VIPs love to get right in, and the average folk feel special by going to an exclusive restaurant where celebrities dine and the wait is longer due to its popularity).

The Four Sisters restaurant in Myanmar doesn't bother with a check. You pay what you think the meal is worth.

Free Advertising With Publicity

Publicity is a great way to reach a lot of people with a limited budget. The key is to have a message that is newsworthy, which obviously changes all the time.
Align With a Charity or Other Non-profit Organization – This is a great way to get free publicity.
Sponsor an event with food or get the local children to come and cook outside.
Be sure to issue press releases with your local newspaper, radio and television stations, and community publications. Stories like these make great humanitarian interest pieces for these media outlets. Who knows? You could be the next guest on Oprah or the Today Show!
Take Time to Get to Know Your Local Editors and Publishers – It's a lot easier to pitch a press release or idea if you already know someone on the inside.

Facebook Marketing

Facebook is certainly one of the biggest internet phenomenons of recent times. It has become so huge that almost all internet users and countless others know about it or use it regularly.

It is for this reason and so many others that internet marketers have jumped on the band wagon and started harnessing it's marketing and selling power for their own gain.

Huge companies like Coca Cola and Nike are making millions of dollars extra per month using Facebook as a marketing tool. But not only the huge companies are harnessing the power of Facebook marketing. Many small business owners, website owners and other internet marketers and people who work from home have discovered how to make money and boost their incomes using Facebook and other social media marketing sites and techniques.

Don't worry if you don't know how to create a fan page or how to use it to market your business. I am going to explain it in easy to follow steps that even a 10 year old would understand.

"Why Facebook?"

As of the first quarter of 2015, Facebook had 1.44 billion monthly active users.

GROUPS OR FAN PAGES?

Well, this is really a no brainer, but it's good to have an explanation of the differences, because each has its own functions.

The best description I've seen is from Mashable: "Groups are great for organizing on a personal level and for smaller scale interaction around a cause. Pages are better for brands, businesses, bands, movies, or celebrities who want to interact with their fans or customers without having them connected to a personal account, and have a need to exceed Facebook's 5,000 friend cap."

SO, WHAT EXACTLY ARE FAN PAGES?

According to the Facebook Pages Manual - which you can download and use for guidance in setting up your Fan Pages - Pages were added to the Facebook milieu so that businesses, organizations, bands, and celebrities could keep in touch with their fans in "an official, public manner."

For us, the key word here is "businesses" because when we use a Fan Page for a niche specific keyword/product, that is our business.

SEARCH ENGINE OPTIMIZATION FOR FACEBOOK
FAN PAGES

There really isn't much difference in the techniques you use for search engine optimization of your Facebook Fan Page than you would use for your blog, or articles, or a website - anything you want to be noticed and indexed for a specific keyword by the search engines. Here are some things to keep in mind when setting up your Fan Page:

1. Go to Google Keyword Tool and enter your main theme keyword and look for additional keywords you can use that have a lot of searches each month. In Google (or Yahoo), you can put in a keyword in quotes (phrase match), to see how much competition there is for pages that use that keyword. Compare the Global Searches Per Month number from the Google Keyword Tool with the number returned by Google and look for keywords for a high number of monthly searches and a low number of competing websites. This will make it easy for you to rank for that particular keyword.

2. Once you have determined your main theme keyword and additional keywords you would like to target, use the main theme keyword in your Fan Page Title and in your Profile.

3. Talk about your Face Page on the Social Networking sites. The most popular ones, aside from Facebook, are hi5, Ning, Bebo, Orkut, Linkedin, Friendster, and MySpace. Use Twitter and Foursquare for microblogging. Do some quality content publishing on various web2.0 sites, such as HubPages, Squidoo, tumblr, Scribd, and ezinearticles. Always, link back to your Facebook Fan Page.

4. In the profiles you create for the different social networking sites, send a link back to your Facebook Fan Page URL.

5. Everybody knows that article marketing is the best way to get your blogs and pages indexed by the search engines quickly. They are great authority sites and the search engines love them.
Write several articles, making sure you use the keyword you want to target both in the article title, description, and the content of the article. In the

resource box at the end of the article, send the viewers back to your Fan Page or, if you have an opt in page on your Fan Page that offers something free that is relevant to the article, send your readers there. Not only will you get indexed quickly, your will begin to build back links to your Fan Page.

Here are some article directories you can use.
URL ----------- Alexa Rating - Google Page rank *
 ezinearticles.com ------- 126 ------------- 6
* articlesbase.com -------- 354 ------------- 6
* suite101.com ------------ 659 ------------- 7
* buzzle.com -------------- 759 ------------- 6
* articlesnatch.com ----- 1,467 ------------- 5
* helium.com ------------ 1,527 ------------- 6
* goarticles.com -------- 1,710 ------------ 4
* articlealley.com ------ 2,200 ------------- 5
* articledashboard.com--- 2,833 ------------ 5
* ideamarketers.com ----- 3,369 ------------- 5
* bukisa.com-------------4,728--------------5
* amazines.com-----------4,759--------------3
* articlecity.com----------5,453--------------5

Some of the article directories are "no follow" but that doesn't matter because, if your articles are well written, they will be picked up by other publishers and published on their blogs, in their newsletters, on their websites, etc., giving your article and link a lot of exposure.

Visit blogs and forums that are relevant to your Fan Page niche, post a useful, helpful comment, and a link back to your Facebook Fan Page.

Those are just some of the ways you can optimize your Facebook Fan Page. Just remember - use your keywords as much as possible and update often to keep your Fan Page "new and interesting", and the search engines will love you!

CREATING YOUR FACEBOOK FAN PAGE

Whether you already have a Facebook profile or not, go to www.facebook.com/pages/ and you will be brought to a page that says "Create a Page."

When you come to the Create a Page screen, you can start by doing the following:

1. Click on "Chose Brand, Products, or Organization"

2. Fill in "Page Name" (make sure to include your main keyword if possible)

3. Click on the box stating you are the official representative.

4. Click "Create Official Page."

If you aren't logged in, or don't yet have an account, you will be prompted at this point to either log in or create an account.

Now it's time to start adding content to your new Fan Page.

The first thing you need to do is add an image for your Page. Pick an image that represents what your Page is about rather than an image of yourself. After you add your photo, you need to edit the thumbnail to make sure it includes the portion of your photo that is most relevant. After the image is uploaded, pass your cursor over the top right-hand corner of the uploaded image. It will open a box with a pencil that says "Change Photo." Click on "Change Photo" and a drop down box will appear. Click on "Edit Thumbnail" and follow the directions to make any adjustments and then click "Save." There is a small box under the photo that asks you to tell something about your Page. Make sure to fill this box out.

Next, click on "Info" tab at the top of the page. On this page, you'll have two fields to add information to, if you wish. The first field is "Basic Info" and basically contains a place to put the date your business was founded.

The second field is "Detailed Information" so you can explain more about your business.

When you finish with these two section, click "Done Editing" and move to the next screen.

Under your photo, you will see "Edit Page." If you click this you will be brought to a section where you can customize your Fan Page however you want to. There are way too many choices to go into all of them here. You need to explore your options and pick the ones that best meet your needs, and the interests of your potential "fans." Once you've created your first Fan Page, it will become increasingly easier to do more pages.

I would suggest you visit the right sidebar. Under "Help with Your Page" is a link "For tips and information about Facebook Pages, click here." Click there and it will take you to a page that will explain everything, under the Resources tab. There is a Quick Start Guide and a Pages Manual that you can download and refer to as you proceed.

Here are some tips to keep in mind:

1. Keep your title short because when you add content your title is added to each post.

2. If you want to, you can chose a "vanity" url after you have twenty- five fans.

3. The maximum size for an image for your Fan Page is 200 pixels (width) by 600 pixels (height). Use the full size if at all possible.

4. Fill out the About Us box right below your picture and include a clickable link back to your main blog, or wherever you choose.

5. Using the application "Social RSS" you can bring your blog posts onto your Fan Page.

6. Let your fans post also on your Fan Page so when someone comes to your page, it looks "alive" with a lot of interaction.

One good thing about Fan Pages is you can send updates, via email to all of your fans at the same time. Not so with your profile page. So, when you have a special article, or a promotion, or some really great information, you can let all of your fans know. Just don't spam them!

If you have set up your SEO properly - putting you keyword in the title and using it elsewhere on your page - when people search for the keyword they will automatically find you. When they do, make sure they find a well- structured, lively page that gives them more than they expected.

If you need help you are welcome to contact the
author Robert Mark Jakobsen
info@markedsoptimering.dk